NIGH

By the same author

The Unlikely Orchard
Suburban Anatomy
Things I've thought to tell you since I saw you last

NIGH

PENELOPE LAYLAND

RECENT
WORK
PRESS

Nigh
Recent Work Press
Canberra, Australia

Copyright © Penelope Layland, 2020

ISBN: 9780648936701 (paperback)

 A catalogue record for this book is available from the National Library of Australia

All rights reserved. This book is copyright. Except for private study, research, criticism or reviews as permitted under the Copyright Act, no part of this book may be reproduced, stored in a retrieval system, or transmitted in any form by any means without prior written permission. Enquiries should be addressed to the publisher.

Cover image: Copyright © Penelope Layland, 2020
Cover design: Recent Work Press
Set by Recent Work Press

recentworkpress.com

SS

For my mother

Contents

NEARLY

The succession of forest trees	3
Lindy	4
Tabula rasa	5
Every single piece of plastic ever made still exists, scientists say	6
Survivalist	7
Somnia	8
Ruin porn	9
Birnam Wood removes, but not to Dunsinane	10
How to demolish a building	11
Voucher specimen	12
Gone in the teeth	14
Geology	16
Shopping list for the sales	17
Volition	18
Sympathy	19
Wisteria	20
Reading the weather	22
Desire lines	23
Alice at the book depository	24
Two Lear limerick centos	25
Having eaten from the tree of knowledge	27
Quaking Aspens, Utah	28
Scintilla	29
Ink	30
The pasts	31
Wanting	35
Unheralded acts of the Gorgon	36
Anzac Parade (the Frontier Wars)	38
Dead letter	39
Naked on the street side	40
Bog people	41
Likenesses	42
The trouble with reading *Nausea* before bed	46
During a blackout	47

NEAR

Jean Miro's birds	51
Uncut pages	52
In the key of C# minor	53
Photographing the orange-bellied parrot	54
Antarctic	55
Caterwaul	56
The toad in the stone	57
Drowned town	58
Kastro, Sifnos	59
Showtime	60
Roaring Forties	63
Blue Poles [Number 11, 1952]	65
West MacDonnell Ranges	66
Good News for Modern Man	67
The sap is rising	68
Fernweh	69
Bogong	70
On a train	72
Monaro swoon	73
After eye surgery	74
Communion	76
Whippet	77
Insatiable	78
The Kats-Chernin	79
Rembrandt	80
Twelfth Night	84
Remaking scenery	85
First and final call	86
Afterword	89

NEARLY

The succession of forest trees

*I am striding on over the fact that it is the earth
that holds our mark longest, that soil dug never returns
to primal coherence.*

Les Murray, *Toward the Imminent Days*

April days become stretched,
and in the forsaken sports stadium at Pripyat
the forest, sewn by irradiated wind,
is deep-rooted now in the pitch, and faintly felted.
Dark buds of maple shake off cold
and new leaves force the last of the old from the oaks.
Rich lichens brocade the silent grandstand.

Drone footage shows wolf eyes flaring white
in the supermarket carpark at night,
brown bears sunning, unconcerned,
on crazed tennis courts,
poplar and aspen prising roof tiles,
rutting bison, necks arched for the roar,
and highways thatched by convulsing vines.

The rotting benches of the stadium
are soft with mossy boils, glistening.
In the city park a rust-blistered Ferris wheel
grates against its stillness.
Tailings of snow lie about, cadmium-white.
Our tilling is everywhere, incoherent,
untrivial, primal as appetite.

Lindy

No suffering but what's deserved,
we said.

These things haunted:
        taut nylon distended in a swift bulge
        red sand flying
        the cello twang of a guy rope
        a mottled mirage of shape
        a scrap flapping
        a small sound.

Our hate was linear as the horizon,
for you were us, in our night terrors,
gasping for the thing we forgot—
unfed, untended.

In whispers, let us relate
how we left her alone
by the unlatched pool gate
with the blind cord in her fat fist
by the lit candle
with the rat poison
and the pill bottle
where the wild dogs are.

Tabula rasa

Sixty harvests until the end of things,
until the last centaur folds from the fetlocks
beside his dry well,
till mermaids shed scales in dulling strips
and wallow in the tepid swell.
The phoenix cannot gather his scattered kindling
in such a wind.
The golden apple splits and turns wormy.
The sphinx has no riddle for the occasion.

The bright poppy, which grows best
in soil assaulted by flash flood or blood,
was no symbol of rebirth and morning, after all,
but a red flag of warning, semaphoring.

Sixty springs of diminishing returns,
then the last leviathan will lie bloated on the beach.
Gone, Gilgamesh, Bruegel's Babel, all of Beethoven,
angels twirling on the bright heads of pins.

Every single piece of plastic ever made still exists, scientists say

A grain in the gut of an albacore or wrass or drummer, or glittering like sand on the gills of the great ray, my loved plastic swan of remembered infant baths drifts her half-life, away from the chlorine and fluoride, at one with the heavy metals.

She dives there with her vector in the mazy deep, with the broken buttons and piano keys that saved the elephants, the Bakelite phone that brought the doctor on the party line, the clingwrap that sealed out the swarming air, the one-use cannulas and Y-sets that saved my cancered sister, the forgotten bags that bore the groceries to our first home together, the scrub that promises me a younger me, sloughed of the old me, sloughed too of the old ways of wood, that denuded the forests.

I cannot swim out far enough into my future to feel exactly the drag or the buoyancy.

Survivalist

It became a trip marker in the crackle of cane fields,
a sign that the beach was not far now.
Buildings of dusty, unchanging carob,
low-slung and windowless,
wind turbines blurring,
a fraying ensign knotted by wind.
All those years of passing by, never any sign of life.

We imagined a dark bunker,
its sacks of dried legumes,
tinned tuna, treacle,
jerrycans of kero and diesel,
ampoules of penicillin,
and for later, seed packets, de-sal rigs,
ammo and oiled rifles
mummified in canvas shrouds.

Our girls have grown, have their own holiday plans.
Last summer we drove west, alone,
across the black-soil plains in locust season,
arriving with an almost clean windscreen.

An actuary would say my chances are good
of outliving the last koala.

Our daughters have no children.

Somnia

Once I slept meagerly,
ate untimely cereal by the bowl,
read numberless pages.

Questions kept me waking:
how to comprehend
the geometry of a wasp's nest

or what bird it was that said
'Oi', 'Oi' in a child's voice
in the secretive scrub?

Now, I read even Derrida
before bed with equanimity,
am satisfied by a description

of the nightingale's song
('a fast succession
of high, low and rich notes')

need no actual notes,
just notes about notes
and a suffix of sleep.

Ruin porn

Walls skinned by spalling,
scalloped as vertebrae with a twist.
Gyprock musty as summer sheets—
3 a.m. and again at 6.
Shadows attach to ambiguous shapes
through windows with no gaze.
There's the squeak, in wind, of a letterbox flap,
a dry rattle of dead snails.
Dark-glossed, the architrave,
with the grease and graze of fingers
almost always unsteady.
A stripped and rotting mattress
is dented in two places
rarely ready.

Birnam Wood removes, but not to Dunsinane

Lion-mettled, we took no care
what chafed or fretted—
as instructed.

Now hubris will be, after all
our fretting fall.

Two trees remain
of Dunkeld's forest—

one oak, prolonged for
theatrical tourism by props,
and one sycamore.

How to demolish a building

Start with the idea of the place,
the glow of it, in late sun, in winter,
its heft, its inked shadows
and the colours, singly and together,
of curtains, some slung to show
interiors impenetrable, or lamplit.

Start with an accounting of
births and deaths, the softly-closed
and slammed doors of leaving,
the bruised, overlapping
sounds of televisions in the night.

Start with the bleed of cigarette smoke,
the sweet music of bottle on glass,
the arrhythmia of pacing footfalls overhead
and names called sharply in the dark.
Start with the fragile spines
of books on shelves or stacked by walls.

Start with beds, with the ripples
made by hips and heads,
the dampness made by the hot flicker
and quick subsidence of dreams.

Use all of these,
and the breaths between,
to estimate
the necessary weight
and speed of the ball.

Voucher specimen

I

Once, perhaps, in a career—a ghost appears,
a jewelled rumour rendered real.
It happened to me:
out of the closed canopy
and into my mist net—a bird careered.

Guadalcanal's mythic kingfisher—the male—
his sapphire back never before described,
his secrets all un-prised, to my eyes a thing
of surmise and legend.

A century ago, one female was seized,
her smokescreen green revealed.
Fifty years later, two more—again, female.
A rattling call had been sometimes heard
but never recorded, rendered real.

He detached from my net, vigorous,
without visible trauma—
came freely to my hand, watchful, alert,
raucous. No other word for it: gorgeous.
You have seen the photographs
in magazines, of course.
He posed, unafraid. Why should he be?

II

In the cloud forest the canopy
is a pierced parasol, all finery and leakage.
Great trunks accrete upwards, slow as stalagmites,
slow-fed by mist and mulch and decay and drip.
I fear they are too rooted, too slow
to outrun man's machinery,
which is always audible at my mind's lip.

For several days, I stare, besotted,
record his glancing, preening quirks,
photograph his crayon streaks,
the speaking orange of his beak,
the impossible, royal plush of his cushioned back.
Then I—collect him.

For a bird of his size
intravenous pentobarbitone is best,
carbon dioxide (in a sealed environment) next.
As far as can ever be assessed, death
is painless, not instantaneous.

Five years on, I can look him in his marble eye
and am not sorry.
I know about sacrifice, statistics, science,
have watched whole, heady, ruddy populations
dwindle to a spark and then vanish.

His gifts to us are multiple and multiply—
molecular, morphological, taxonomic.
Then, there was his exoticism,
his cuteness appeal, his political possibility—
forgive me—the blue, ruffling, diverting jewel
of his never-before-seen plumage.

Gone in the teeth

White coated, he spoke
through unsmiling canines
to tell me it could not be saved.
It was levered out with a crunch
no louder than cornflakes
and I went back to my life for a while.
But it changed things—
made me tentative
around apples and toffee
and toffee apples.
And I now seem to notice more
the rough red on the backs of hands
that never quite heals,
the percussion of shoulders,
the blear that won't be blinked away,
and unseasonal cicadas.
A patter of aberrations,
polite at first
but at night becoming
a thudding on wood.

Lavender Bay

for Brett Whiteley

Owning such a window I would, like you,
have endlessly looked through
its white framing—sometimes kiltered to a wind-eye,
other times capsuled against gales
or kaleidoscopic with running rain.

In that frame, the harbour dun-coloured in lush rain;
or matte orange in scalding sunfall;
or blue—so see-through
that sand shows canvas-clean here,
while—just there—you wallow, lapis-lazuli-saturated
in Renaissance adoration.

Wendy's sharp hipbone is suggested
in everything,
and three inches from everything,
always hard up against rapture,
the depths are a drum-cracking Slessor black.

Geology

In another life I am a geologist and still possess the fist of obsidian
a grandfather fossicked from the Mount Warning shield—
scalloped facets of toffeed treacle, impenetrably dark.

I kept my rocks in a shoe-box shod with cotton wool,
not comprehending then that durability could be conjoined to beauty:

my slippery obsidian; a rubble of cooking-disaster conglomerate;
a slip of geode bristling with sparks of amethyst;
a knob of cold, alien hematite; and a fossil trilobite
levered from rock barely harder than clay
and losing its lustre within a day.

At some point my box was lost—given or thrown away
along with dreams of lava tubes, tectonic restlessness,
thin soils creamed from gravel paddocks by summer winds.

I imagine a scattering in rehabilitated landfill somewhere:
box and cotton long decayed, just my rocks,
clustered in unlikely proximity, re-writing the laws of geology.

Shopping list for the sales

Skirt, of a length neither slutty nor dowdy, suitable for funerals or work (trans-seasonal). Those stay-up stockings that do. White shirt cut for the small-breasted, not see-through. Ditto, red, see-through. Remaindered books by Eastern European authors. Orange linen t-shirt that will make me sallow and won't wash well. Cloche I will immediately regret and put in the charity bin, then immediately regret putting in the charity bin, already sick for what I had, or do not yet have, or cannot have.

Volition

Ag-science in a city school is for dummies
not farmers' sons,
but even we knew enough to laugh
at the girl who believed trees could
shake a glad leaf, stretch a cramped limb,
if the notion took them.

It took me years to see
the mis-planted pear reach for light
round the southern wall, the pencil pine
shimmy off cold into the wind,
the straggled photinia beckon its share of bees,
and the big old street trees bow low
in great, sultry shudders
in the heat of midday.

And what tiny shrieks, beyond hearing,
from those radish shoots cocooned
in labelled test tubes
on the classroom sill?
Did they not flinch at the campaign of attrition—
the daily swill of vinegar or bleach—
that the teacher might teach
of human volition,
mastery, over-reach?

Sympathy

The more I feel
the more I have room
for no-one.
My womb jerks away
from babies
with starfish hands and
startled eyes
being passed
over high fences.
My chest is caged against
the women on my screen
whose arms, released
of their burdens
fly upwards in distress.
My ardour shrivels
from the menfolk who
having lost all, want
something in their fist.
I am not strong
enough for this.

Wisteria

In wind, the pendulous wisteria groans,
its own showiness grown unbearable
till its flowers lie, acid-purple heaped,
and its bines reveal their true age
which is grey and twisted and stiff,
whatever new green would have you think.

Beauty is blunted by wind—think
of the woman who, alone in the dark, groans
as she turns again, and now again, stiff
with wear and the unbidden, unbearable
notion that spring is just another old age
with painted slapper face, colours heaped

on, but interim as soft wisteria skin, heaped.
The bines climb clockwise. Do you think
they think on this? And what age
—guess—is the woman who groans
at her own sleeplessness, at the unbearable
insistence of the bedside clock, her stiff

fingers now silencing its clangour? The stiff
window latch grudges air, her things are still heaped
where dropped, the mirror is unbearable.
To think, she thinks, to think...
but what it was eludes her reflection. She groans
as she gathers her underthings, whose age

is grey and grubbied lace. But at her age,
who but the wind might whistle, grow stiff
against her garments, the wind that groans
among heavy-hung wisteria, among heaped
flowers flung down? To think
a season cannot beg a delay is unbearable.

The breakfast radio is unbearable
in its brightness, the kettle takes an age
to drown it out with whistling. You think
she thinks on this? Or drinks her tea, standing stiff
at the sink, leaves the dishes heaped
there, tries the tap, which groans,

tries to think in degrees of unbearable:
to go, through wind that groans, through light that shows her age,
or to stay, sit awhile beneath stiff bines, their purple heaped?

Reading the weather

Ultrasoundings are masses of murk
in oceans of black, where everything
that's a gallbladder has the stenotic pulse
of a stuttering heart
while the placid unborn
swim, capsuled, like dead amphibians.
Cirrus clouds drift beneath the wand
as actual clouds do actually drift,
though clouds here are punctuated
by crisp crosses embossed
by the technician
who measures angles and thicknesses
and the distances between things
like eyes and noses
and the circumferences of any niggling
or any asymptomatic masses.
Back, forwards, backwards, like
the weather-man's hand before
the greenscreen, conjuring isobars.
Peering at clouds it is easy to suppose
that fine weather lies dead ahead,
or the exact opposite.

Desire lines

Given a chance we walk aslant,
offside, on the grass,
leaving marks of passing.
 We are carvers of petering scars,
 makers of holes in hedges,
  forgers of flowerless tracks
  through garden beds.
   We braid oceans with our
   momentarily fomenting wakes
   and crack fresh snow as though
   nothing could be injured beneath.
    We beat away till the clay shows,
    fraying summer lawns,
     fretting and terracing slopes
     with steps that go toward
     and away from.
      We are the wisdom of the crowd,
      the ego of the short-cut.

Alice at the book depository

Why is a raven like a writing desk? Because both blacken mood (whatever the mood). Because a moulted or pulled quill, whetted and loaded to the gills with ink, makes the glowing deskplace a workspace and the bird denuded. Because goose, swan, turkey, eagle, owl and hawk can be elevated, though not necessarily, by uplift, by a voice lifting from a white page, as a lark might.

Two Lear limerick centos

1.

2nd lines only, as interrogatives

Who looked out at the depths of the Night?
Who was troubled with horrible dreams?
Who held up his hands in amazement?
Who said, 'I'm afloat! I'm afloat'?

Who wept, when the weather was murky?
Who shrank from sensations of cold?
Who walked on the tips of his toes?
Who was always polite to all ladies?

Who shut his wife up in a box?

Who divided his jugular artery?

Who swept the loud chords of a lyre?

Who wished he had never been born?

2.

4th lines only, as tragedy

To drinking, he took.

And their conduct was such
he rode wholly away
to examine the sea.

He fell into the water—
they said he was drowned,
fished him out with a hook
with his feet in the air,
with his head in a sack.

She ceased to repine.
She enraptured the deep
and said calmly—'This comes',
and called out—'Who's afraid?'

Every evening in June
when the weather was calm
all the birds in the air
—four Larks and a Wren—
filled her heart with despair.

Some, she drowned at the pump.

Having eaten from the tree of knowledge

Once, comets were portents of ruined seasons, ruddy mildews, straining ewes with conjoined lambs jammed, and sand palms—their parched hands and tinder skirts taken by pouncing flame. Now, we can augur the hour of the comet's arrival at our horizon, know it nothing but a brittle boulder of ice and grit, trailing its own boiling essence, unreachable by prayer.

Quaking Aspens, Utah

Whispers lap, layered as a waterfall
even in breeze so low it can scarcely be called so,
rising to ring out in higher winds like
the clash of minted coins falling.

We have come to lie at feet that are not feet
any more than branches are limbs
—but we can only call things by words we know,
and what grows below the skin of earth
is below our thinking,
as what goes on inside our lying skin
is below an aspen's thinking.

The whispers we have come to hear
say nothing—are just fancies, like those breakers
that crash from an empty conch.
The aspen's whispers are simply, strictly,
struck by the wind's thumb that is not a thumb
—and say nothing.

What sense is spoken is spoken underground—
along shallow, sunless roots that reach and knit
and where coded messages run—
the monologue of a monstrous clone
communing with its forty thousand selves,
each saying what is already known,
laid down in its horny fossil of memory

—how to embrace stasis before snow
then how to wake again—and speaking
as a heart speaks with a head on matters more immediate:
where to sucker next; what ageing self to sacrifice;
where pine and goat and fire have encroached;
on which hillside sun will shine.

Scintilla

The blank surface wakes to a slow roil of lips and flanks
as the carp rise from suspension.

From bridge-height it's a blistering that suddenly stretches whale-wide
and moves with one brain, many mouthed.

I have seen koi meander skewbald in dimpled pools
in light French rain,
and purse coyly at a scatter of crumbs on the algal meadow
of an Indian step well.

Now I am taught they are unbeautiful,
feral and mud-breathed.

Yet as the warmth hits, they are lit, ecstatic, metallic,
squirming for purchase in a silt-yellow column of light.

Ink

She's inscribing texts on her arms in needled ink, serif font, starting with Kerouac, from there to Woolf, Plath. As an infant, dandled naked and trusting on my hip, her arm brushed a radiator in deep Canberra winter, raising in an instant a field of ripe blisters, poised for wet blossoming. Each nudge, burn, break, caress, embrace, slip, slap, stitch, incision, leaves its protective carapace on skin. Ink alone is chosen, not chanced, eloquent, not delinquent.

The pasts

Leaving Istanbul, the train idles for a signal change
at a cutting of dense and cluttered reds and whites:
conglomerate of shells, trinkets, trash and shards,
pasts compressed by this urgent present,
each present overbuilding the last.

Between me, in my stalled carriage,
and Byzas, obedient to the Oracle,
just eighty generations, each flattened
in compactus with the generations beneath—
triumphs, bloodings, memory of love,
prayers of the remnant, brickwork revenant,
pelt of carpet, velvet of dog,
broken tiles and broken teeth.

From the cold lap of the Bosphorus
the generations rise in one midden-mound
to the haggling market of the present present,
more trinkets and trash in the making.

Eighty lifetimes—close enough
for an amphora to smell of the wine it held,
for a bone to resurrect a festive meal
or speak of unnatural death.
Above the cutting and already sunk to its ankles,
a wall, horny and scalloped as a tortoise shell,
punctured every three metres by air-conditioning units
glittering like revealed tesserae.

Taphophobia variations

The earth is suffocating.... swear to make them cut me open, so that I won't be buried alive—Frédéric Chopin.

I

It was his sister, Ludwika, who saw to it.
Bobbing in cognac, his heartwood
was smuggled past Russian border guards
(who, in the cindery railway dark,
may not have known one meat from another)
to Warsaw, there to be bricked, beatless,
still in its crystal flask,
in a church pillar, forever,
or for however long forever lasts.

II

In the span of a few generations,
embalming and cremation
have nuanced the ancient horror.
No-one survives phenol, ethanol,
glutaraldehyde infused with rosy dyes.
Fire, either, though recent photographs
may serve as guides
to ensure the parting of your hair
or lipstick hue
do not make you stranger
to those who—even knowing
what happens next—
need you, for this afternoon,
to look as though you might still be alive.

III

In 1995 a patent was granted
for a computer-age re-interpretation
of the Safety Coffin.
Included in the retail price: intercom, alarm,
long-life torch, compact breathing apparatus
and heart monitor/starter (combined).
Absent, certain features deemed essential
by earlier patent-holders and their clientele—
glass panes for observation,
marionette strings for fingers and toes
leading upwards to monitored bells,
even rope ladders, for the more athletic revivals.
Also, water, dried fruits, cigarettes, port—
grave offerings from the soon-to-be-resumed world.

IV

For his Dead Christ in the tomb
the Younger Holbein used as a model
a corpse from the Rhine.

The canvas is unconventional.
We pry, edge-wise, into a
coffin-sized, suffocating space.
No need for patented contrivance here—
this, evidently and without contradiction,
is no body buried alive.
The eyes and mouth are slackly opened,
though not to see and speak—
the hands and feet are dark with dissolution.

A honeymooning Dostoevsky
stood before it, transpierced,
till dragged clear by his wife.
Later, he will have his pure Prince, Myshkin
stand similarly fixed by

faith's tormenting, insatiable need
to constantly confront itself
with what it would deny.

Wanting

It was winter, so any thought beyond
the memory of warmth was extravagant.
You told me this. I did not listen.

When the wattle eructed and smells headied
from the wet soil you said,
'best be sure of what we really want'.

The fires, that summer, drove before them anything still living.

I am crisp and soluble as an autumn pinoak leaf, gripping,
and unable, without catastrophe, to ungrip.

Unheralded acts of the Gorgon

1. Pompeii

Having left the leaving too late, the merchant is fixed
in the act of his rising—or trying—
through a rain of pyroclastic ash, the
milky boilover of her poison breath.
His arm is a lever against familiar, solid earth,
his back tensed against newborn, airborne earth that hisses.

Others are fixed foetally in family sets, or alone:
an infant seemingly in the act of learning to crawl;
an abandoned dog, urgent against its leash.
For each, a slim sarcophagus of hollowness,
cindery bones fallen into negative space,
a figure-ground reversal, at once vase and face.

2. Lark Quarry

Jump-up country, all lancewood, spinifex
and those painted finches, splashed and flashy
with crimson and white, blinking against
the throbbing scarp. Of that other day
there remains only a chaos of footprints arrested
upon the turning earth in the instant of the stampede.

A herd, bird-footed, sabre-fanged,
on a day of spore-drowsy ferns, clubmoss
and great, ragged claws of nimbus
blackened with their own sodden portent.
On the breathless mudflat, smoothed for their sgraffito,
the adults look riverward at her sudden scent.

3. *Whitby*

The North Sea, on a day of bluster, picks and prises
black jewels from the seams of jet slabbed
in the cliff-face, to be fossicked, scraped
and burnished into trinkets to mourn the dead.
Rubbed on sleeve or heart, lignite ignites, sends sparks.
The wood still speaks from its long compression—*burn me.*

So long deprived of sap and light, it cannot recall
how its fist of roots wrestled a hundred seasons' storms,
how its limbs were slow-skinned by seasons of ice.
But its stone grain records the toppling, the encroaching water,
the smothering silt, her hair a crown in high wind, writhing,
her face, full-on, petrifying.

Anzac Parade (the Frontier Wars)

Something revenant melts behind a blue gum,
wobbles un-named in the deepest shade.
But the enemy can never be shown here,
lest he take a human frame.

Conjure then, in this numinous space,
a lean man, striking chips from a flint,
a woman with a palmful of blackish berries,
a girl, kneading a gift of flour for the flames.

In each freeze-frame, a diegesis:
Coniston Creek, at Brooks Soak, near Alice,
a decade after the war to end wars,
in the year my father was born.

Blood Hole, Mount Dispersion, Cape Grim,
Fighting Hills, Butchers Creek,
Slaughterhouse Gully, Convincing Ground,
Murderers Flat, Rifle Creek.

Placenames providential, consonant, or a simple freak,
but without resonance, less familiar
to hot, bored students even than Amiens,
Passchendaele, Menin Road, Ypres.

Every day here is Unremembrance Day,
each fractal massacre a fraction
of a crystallising pattern
that disappears into our wallpapering.

On the avenue it has been hell-hot this summer.
Substrate tar bubbles blackly through the gravel.
Hot beads sit on the surface
like tumours on pale skin.

Dead letter

No answer is no answer,
so I wrote to the poles to you
and my letters never came back.

It lets me think there's a chance,

lets me think of my words warm
in your heart's pocket,
tone softened from folding and unfolding,
less scolding,

not lying uncracked
in some facility somewhere,
all that heat, that hate, turning incendiary.

Naked on the street side

How was it she had never noticed the manoeuvre by which
he switched and re-switched so it was always he, not she,
at risk of the arc of water, oil and grit played upward
from the passing tyre, to drench his trouser leg, again?

The sleight of hand as he handed her, handled her,
steered her by her elbow, like a surgeon manipulating
a remote machine, a flensing knife or similarly subtle
instrument of kind correction.

And her nylons thanked him.
Her high, beige, suede heels thanked him.
Her dry-clean-only-ness thanked him.

Now, she walks as one winged—feeling unclipped.
The hairs flinch up from her forearm, naked on the street side.

Bog people

They earn our gaze only by resistance to disintegration, the miracle of a withered pap, concave cheek, a still decipherable tattoo. A high sodium reading, an absence of scavenging animals, will do it for you, too.

We are all preserved temporarily in memory's wet weave and love's compression and the aridity of grief. Each with desiccated ligature, tannin-tanned limb, shriveled tumour, preserved fracture. Fossil baby in fossil womb. It's the startle of recognition that makes them special. The instant-eternity of it. Choke or starve. Brutal short.

Likenesses

1.

Illuminate

(Saigon, June 11 1963)

All I could think was, the subject illuminated itself.

I could work that cheap, Japanese Petri
in the dark or in my sleep:

aperture/focal length/focus
clickclickclickclick/reload/clickclick

The gathered monks were mostly just boys.

Some cried out.

I used ten rolls, shooting non-stop.

You can see the car boot, still open,
where the jerrycan was stashed.
One monk placed a cushion on the road,
one monk removed the cap.

Afterwards, there was the business
of getting the exposed film safely away.

We used a 'pigeon' booked on a regular flight,
convinced to slip something extra in his carry-on.

From the Manila bureau
pictures could go worldwide, by radio.

I only knew for sure the film was through
when the messages of congratulation began to arrive.

2.

Predator

(South Sudan 1993)

Small sounds alerted me.

Infant—no—*infantalised,*
made big-headed by hunger.
On buckled knees
hooped barrel of chest
face grounded as if praying.

As I chose my lens the vulture lit,
unshuttered, utterly focused.

I waited twenty minutes for it
to unwind its wings,
give me my even greater drama.   It didn't.

Compression of distance,
manipulation of depth of field
would need to be enough.   It was.

Protocols for foreign media forbade
physical contact with locals,
to limit disease transmission.

Just to be clear,
I chased it away afterwards.

3.

No filter

(Paris, 31 August 1997)

I was first. Technically.

On the scene, I mean,
though with no camera on me.
My job was to tail them
—faster on two wheels—
and let the snapper know by radio
which way to go.
My man was there quickly.

Later, it was decreed
by French precedent:
the inside of a car
is as sacrosanct
(as regards privacy)
as a boudoir.

So, no money shot.
No film noir.

Well, je ne comprend pas.
It was game on, that night—
always game, always on.

Just the way she wanted it.
Lashes, blushes, flashed thighs, glances,
coded coyness—*Jesus*—
she was the honeypot
and we knew it.

So did you, who bought the rags, the mags,
hung on every pixilated kiss.

First was first, and first was always money.
Oh, honey,
always perfect in the frame—
it was a grand game, wasn't it, love?

The trouble with reading *Nausea* before bed

I have dreamed for a living.
If I had imagined
this was how it would be
I would never have begun,
would instead have drunk
Pastis or pesticide,
thrown dice, spun barrels,
slept with more men
who were not the one.
When I lift my hair in the heat,
I smell insecticide in my pits.
When I roll over, my flesh
follows in a slovenly wave.
I cannot recall my last dream.
This morning my pen makes
marks that are indistinguishable
from a shopping list.

During a blackout

I write this
by headlamp
which heightens drama,
pushes back dark
in white, depthless arcs
when I turn my head,
which means
I turn my head
more and more
write less and less,
watching instead
the indoor phosphor
sky of my making
and hearing
the rubble
of air out there
hitting things,
hearing
the ostinato rain.
The poem
I was going to write,
which was about love,
coils and sleeps again.

NEAR

Jean Miro's birds

Sometimes his birds are fish
or have a shark's drawn-
down chinlessness
or are arch as cats on branches
or *are* branches
or Uffington horses,
in the way
that these other things
are also birds—
fish, because they too fly
in swelling murmurations,
on currents, in
choreographed sympathy;
the shark, because,
suffocating incidental
in some predatory net
she makes the same wild
and silent gape
as the yellow bird
yawning to death in the shaft;
the cat, because both sleep
with eyes slit
anywhere the sun hits;
the branch, because either
against winter-white sky
is clear cold nakedness;
the chalk horse because
both are imagined beings,
hollow-boned, hand-cut,
throbbing with the instinct for flight.

Uncut pages

Salvaged from his relic things,
I iron my father's handkerchiefs.

I iron them as my mother did:
squared flat in two balletic sweeps
then folded—swept—folded—swept—

a closing out of the just-lived week,
a making, from its small remains,
provisions for the next.

Gulp of steam, hot cotton swoon,
a rhythmic rock on naked heels,
a pleasure in precision.

Stacked and cooling in my drawers,
the best, least-frayed, are kept for worst—
the days when it is dark by noon.

The rest, for fleeter days like this,
small books with uncut pages where
all my thanks is written.

In the key of C# minor

As silence tightened
he crouched at the keys,
one end of the dowel wet
between right molars,
the other pushing hard,
marking the piano case
with small scars.

Each felted hammer-fall
rang in jawbone,
tooth, temple,
bypassing the ruined drum.

Trauermusik for a slow descent—
left-hand lament; right-hand chant.

The sound the moon makes
poured on an inked lake,
as heard by a low-skimming bird
heading fast and hard
and hopeless into the blank.

Photographing the orange-bellied parrot

At Melaleuca, two of the last 30 alight,
two metres to my right.
My seeing,
I know,
cannot save them—
that meteor has already struck.
They touch sticky beaks across a gap of branch
in a lithium ion blanch.
I carry the codex for nine days through mud.
Two years on, it roosts in my hard drive,
format soon to be superseded,
undownloadable.

Antarctic

The horizon of the albatross is not fixed,
as that of the landbird,
into a settled, navigable matrix.
Mountains vulcanise each ash-grey moment
and crumble in foam and thunder.
The caldera yawns, wet as jaws,
then blinks black, blandly opaque.
The air too is alpine, solid with stress:
peaks bulge and peter beneath
pivoting, fingering wings.
Surviving such tumult means seeking no harbour,
expecting no succour,
giving weight fully to the wind.

Caterwaul

At night, my blind cat caterwauls
and paces tight tracks
on the timber floor,
shedding transparent, hooked
layers of claw
that once would have been flayed
on tree-bark, fence-post or rat-spine
but are now deposited,
small, clear capsules,
in the barricaded rooms
she still stalks.
I never knew this—about the claws—
till now, when we both spend
so much time at home.

The toad in the stone

Consider the toad in the stone,
chipped free from its solitude,
freed into the unknown
from a marble tomb
that armoured each moist limb,
acid skin sculpting its own vault,
heart slowed till each pulse became tidal,
a slow wash from the stone-
cold of inner space.
There, alone, anomalous,
the toad meditated long on meaning:
why a wart is ugly, a starlet's mole not;
when cold-blooded came to mean cold,
and warm-blooded hot?
How old, the toad, how long alone,
till bashed by blunt trauma
free of its trance it vaulted
instinctively into abundance,
unused muscles feebly unbalanced,
third eyelid, slick as a camera shutter,
sealing from the awful,
the suddenly teeming air.

Drowned town

In the sixth year of dry
the dam shrank from its margins
towards the spillway,
became a denser, flocculant green.
Silt banks drifted,
the wind rubbed free outlines
of pitted kerbing, rubbled roads,
brick stumps that once propped
a hardwood floor,
a rack of ginger beer bottles,
cheeks corked against the air.
Emergent from the slub:
a baby blanket, folded
into dissolving tissue;
a tannined teapot,
scattered like a hatched egg;
a sludge of books with blurred corners;
a doll's head, with a crest
of sulphur yellow;
headstones, tilting and slurried;
a small bird perched on a gable,
twig snagged in its beak.

Kastro, Sifnos

It becomes our habit to inhabit
briefly the small cool cells
of white-wash, blue-domed
walls igloo-thick
to test the weight of
weathering doors
that always permit.

It is morning or afternoon
the spring chill the same
standing, adjusting
on the doorway's tongue of flame
till the dark softens
smelling of unmoved dust
and the hot heaviness
of the single votive taper
drilled by hand in a basin
of sand, burning as if
lit moments earlier
by no-one we ever see
its flame merely flinching
from the breeze of our arrival.

Showtime

1.

With neck of swan, nostril of aristocrat,
the alpacas balance like amputees
on feet as small as kitchen knobs.
The flattened turf is slicked in swirls
as they pirouette away
from white-coated handlers.

Lashes flutter as felted sashes
are knotted around
their taut and dipping necks,
like scarves in this season's colours.

2.

Dahlias erupt in arrested pyrotechnics
and folded fractals of implausible origami.
Medusa, beach-blonded,
and mad granny hair in chemical violet.

Roses, beheaded for beauty and propped singly,
nod now on the warning pickets
of their own savage stems,
all hope of victory abandoned.

3.

After three days of 30 degrees
the mock cream is mocking cream,
resembles grout, but dirtier.

In the Basic Sponge Cake display,
cut surfaces pinch parched lips inward.
On flimsy, thumb-stained card:
Commended: Packet Cake: Iced on Top Only.

4.

The men are large and dark as bark
but fidget like seamstresses
as they knock nails, neat as pins,
into the crowns of their blocks
with the heels of bright axes.

Their faces, beef-red, buckle in the mirrored metal.
The first two strikes will be uppercuts
at the jugular.
A big man swivels slowly from the hips,
breathing like a discus thrower
on display in his small circle.

5.

The science of displaying a guinea pig
demands a deft, two-handed gesture
that synchronously scoops, smooths,
tucks tiny feet and elbows away
and leaves on show
a bullet of flesh with small, red eyes.

The judges employ the same palpation
to test the fullness of shoulders,
the compactness of belly and hips.
A gloved finger retracts the lips
to examine the wear pattern on teeth.

6.

Not even the blowflies dare settle on the Santa Gertrudis,
sleek steak, with a fluid ripple under the skin
and the swinging weight below.

Knows he could send things sideways, if he liked—
that woman with the clipboard, that trestle,
the slither of ribbons,
the slim girl at the end of the rope.

Roaring Forties

Wind hustles us along
miles of cambered sand.
Oystercatchers jab
perfect exploratory tubes
and stay ever head-on
to the onrush of air.
Their feathers do not even fluff.
Rounding the headland, wind comes at us
at once from every way,
shearing deadweight breakers to fine spray,
blizzarding sand to mist,
fixing us in a storm eye,
our packs suddenly light
as boulders sucked to the sky.

Pobblebonks
(at Yarrangobilly thermal spring)

The creek emerges kettle-hot from its hearth-stone
to be leveed, pool-shaped, quickly cooled
by a mouthy winter sky.

Ice still numbs those higher streams
where galaxias poise, inert,
clenched to the memory of sun.

Here, steam drifts with its promise of warmth,
though skin flinches at the very idea.
I swim, because to swim I have come.

Thickets of tadpoles swarm and veer as one
from my trawl-net of hair, my wan Gargantua,
ungainly, ungilled, chilled.

Small fry jostle in each of their phases—
pinpoint hearts in jellied scum,
brief black commas, head-heavy infants,

the knee-jerking, handless ones,
the warty froglets, readying,
sipping at the dry strangeness of sun.

The pool is dammed by a spillway
that the strong will grasp and heave upon,
dropping into the creek below

to rehearse their heart-pumped,
time-stamped sexy drum,
their bonking, sounding banjo.

Blue Poles [Number 11, 1952]

I'm lost in dense bush
seeking a register
of familiarity:
the mandarin of flame,
white of bled light,
cold char black.
There's a harmonic
of invisible birds:
lucid bell, bleb of whip,
the mimic lyre.
Son of Wyoming
somehow
knowing
how spears of tree-fern cock, here,
how a skin of clay splits
and lifts.
How hot resin,
burst from bark,
like paint, runs and clots.

West MacDonnell Ranges

In the sharp quartzite litter
that bruises and hobbles my feet
I seek what all seek—
the glimpse, the sharper glitter

of a geode cracked egg-open
and spilling its store of light.
It seems important I find it,
not for the find—which, broken,

will be murky with occlusions
like a succulent after a storm,
matted with debris, transformed
into ordinary—but the delusion.

Good News for Modern Man

Paperback, as befits a people without genealogy.
Plain of speech, pared of pith. Big print.
It dispensed with the rosary, was
dispensed at the grocery.

'Thought for thought, not word for word'
was what it taught, or tried to.
Bold white cover, with blocked vermillion,
it outsold Spock in the age of the Pill,
the advent of which came too late
for our mother, whose exhaustion delivered us,
some random Sundays, to a rented hour
in a weekday classroom of banana skins and dust,
and a nice young man in a cardigan.

But how could such plain prose accounts
ever hope to touch us, with our side-smirks,
our eyes flirting, even in prayer?
How, with the caroling magpies
and their holy hosannas through the glass,
with the incense of sun-showers on asphalt
and slashed summer grass, with our
small, stubborn ounce of antipodean poetry?

The sap is rising

Spring is for tallying, for knowing
which and how many trees
are still numbed in a winter
from which they will not come back.

In these first weeks it is guess-work—
sloth, late slumber or true juicelessness?
Bark, still unparched, dense and warm
in its gloving lichen, gives no sign of which,

and the birds perch, survey and preen regardless.
But the sap is rising in us—
the tallying of opportunities
and immense costs.

After the ease of winter's inner stillness
unresolved things now press for attention.

Fernweh

Before first light the koel keens, lamenting still as afternoon thunder shudders in from the west.

Sadness is infectious. The female feels the compass needle wobble in her heart as she deposits her single egg in a mudlark's perfect pottery bowl. She will be long gone north when her jeweled gift cracks open its infant gape, a matador's irresistible red cape.

Afternoon storms decay the perfect nest, lash by lash, while the mudlarks pitch in the wind, unpreened, in thrall to the unappeasable.

Bogong

It's a trap.
Long, warm corridors of waxy wood
become a dusty smother,
a panic of friable wing,
a beating on, an over-crawling,
adherent as scales
battening to the warm, pale, vaulting walls
while the starry ensign cracks and roils above,
tugging at its tripod mast,
proclaiming country, shredding.

> *Sleep, cutworm,*
> *screwed deep in the blacksoil plains.*
> *Wake, urgent with dreaming*
> *of alpine caves,*
> *of lying in cooler darkness among your millions*
> *like a spotted cloak of barely breathing feathers,*
> *beautiful as the bat,*
> *fragile as the moss.*

Fly-by-night, mistake the light
of the ensign for dawn,
spiral down, seek shade and sleep,
the cool, the crevice.
Find instead a labyrinth
built to hold Minatour and moth.
Blind-batter in books,
nosing upskirting for the damp
and dark. Disintegrate
on the cutting edge of metal shafts
the slip and squeak of parquetry,
the trick of all those windows
with their fine pollen dusting of wing.

Drabber than the butterfly, less preening.
Drag out from the blacksoil,
dry your damp wings, set course for the mountains
you hold in your ancient heart,
the spare, cool caves, above the treeline
where all life is small and scrubby and particular as you.

I shriek, mornings,
at the out-of-placeness in this built place,
the small, sad softness, the persistence.
In a meeting I open my papers
and three fly,
cling to calves, inner thigh.
As I leave, evenings,
seagulls circumnavigate the flagmast,
gorging in a white, scrappy eddy
against the navy sky.

On a train

One day soon on the early train
I'll hand you the poem
of your upper lip
and the point where your neck slips
into the clasped hands of your collar.
I will have words for
the wash of your irises,
the way you wear
traces of weeping
in the tired, inflamed places.
I will tell you about your hands
and the yellow light
and what they perfect together.
It is unspoken,
but I know that one morning
will be our last
and though I cannot predict which one,
I can prepare.
I do not know your name.
You do not look my way.
You never look my way.
You'll not read my poem.
I'll not write it,
I'll never write it.

Monaro swoon

Going south, windows down.
Late autumn puddles its coolness in dips,
like the chill mists that congeal and grip
beneath a river's sunlit skin.

Beige plains are thrown forward—
mile on mile of softened pleats,
my heart's unmattressed, threadbare sheets.

Gold is sallowed by gradual inching
as dark pinches a creeping path
up hills that, while the light still lasts,
are a roller-coaster for eyes.

After eye surgery

Something is on the hill.

A Viking barrow? Modern art?
Something that lives—a tree maybe?

The back of my eye has torn adrift.
Though they've blanket-stitched it
back to bed it's a wait-and-see—or not-see—
while the receptors glitch,
and no certainty that what I see
as beauty isn't actually a bit of a bitch.

All now is molten, dazzling,
a central writhe with an aureole spangling—
a Francis Bacon in every frame.

So I make of things, and hills, what I will.
Ants swill the pages of any text,
exotic arabesques of cédille and circonflexe
attach to the plainest of shopping lists.
The computer screen is a small, silent
for-my-eyes-only discotheque.

In a meeting, a man I detest
slides into a never-resolving puddle.
My sister's face bloats
into a mirror-mazed muddle and she's
drunk-ogre laughing as I tell her
how she looks, which is pretty, in a way,
as well as pretty ugly.

I cover my good eye, stare deep into the fracturing.
It has been a year and the hills are as clear
as the hills are ever going to get.

Well and good: what was ever on the hill?
A barren fell or a forest felled?
Always a guess. Beauty, mostly—or at best.
It's all about perspective.
By which I mean mindset.

Yet I am afraid.
I keep asking, what's on the hill?
Knowing, even as I ask, and whatever I am told,
that I am now beholden,
for things once casually beheld.

Communion

Every instant, I just miss. The one who left the sachet twist at my café table and whose body heat remains in my seat. The one who stood, just here, smoking a still-vivid cigarette. The one who palped this pomegranate with five fingertips but replaced it in the ruddy pile, or left trace perfume in this lift, or last returned this library book from the floor beside a bed.

My mother frets at names mis-said: second cousins, book-club titles, the Minister for This or That. She is brightened when I remind that we are evolved for hearth-groups, not the metropolis—for acquaintances numbering fewer than a hundred, even fewer of them dear, a handful of plots, told and re-told. Yet in my heart I am enraptured by the never-met, the name never-shaped in my mouth, the heat in the seat, the book to be read, and here on the ground, deposited a moment ago, a fragile cylinder of ash the size of a stranger's drawn breath.

Whippet

Built for speed and for the love of it,
his sprung ribcage grazes the grass
as he turns, re-turns
full torque, then pivoting on dancer's toes,
slithers to stillness, doe-eyed
beneath dipped lashes.

So lean, each planned movement
shows as preparatory flinch,
a nervous system current-struck,
each breath a visible lung
bellowing to be fed,
each heart-beat a flicker in his neck.

There's delight in his quick glance—at me—
as the other dogs, bred for doggedness,
or brains, or flatness of face
fail, furiously, to keep pace.
He pirouettes past, sinking at the last
in a perfect plie, like a nesting swan.

Good dog, two years gone.

Insatiable

Phantom exits the final frame with horse and hound, leaving only this page of smudgy sells for sea monkeys, money boxes with combination locks, promise of proficiency on the mouth organ in 30 minutes. Never did send for the x-ray spectacles, sachets of stamps from a guaranteed 20 nations. No habit of purchase, but insatiable belief even now and nevertheless in the phantom potential of a tiny spy camera, its imagined spools of thread-like film, girl genius solves at last the baffling crime, the x-ray reveal of a best friend's parasitic twin notched shriveled in her liver, the amazed face of my mother at my sudden musicality, insatiable even for the cellophane packs of small stamps, mainly maroon, bearing palm trees, public buildings with shaded colonnades and king-like turbaned heads.

The Kats-Chernin

The Kats-Chernin is a bristle
of hand-written accidentals
shaken and spilled into the stave.

To practice alone is to tempt hysterics,
despair, physical injury.
Where is the key?
Signature?
Melody?

Where?

Until the first rehearsal—
then we cleave
and everything collides,
magnetic parts
tossed from firsts to
seconds and back
to the cello
across a bridge of filled air.

Rembrandt

1.

An issue, for the self-portraitist,
is the revelation of others
with a hand or stake or trace
in the face's creation—

the one, for example, whose beauty
brought you first undone
who kissed your lips into bud
and then left you suddenly done for

or worse than.
Where is she in your shifting,
your mutability—the nose that
coarsens or sharpens mood to mood,

hair from wire to silk to brush,
skin from boyish flush
to pitted and brutal,
eyes fox-dark to drilling?

At whom do you gaze, now with
complacency, now contempt?
The invisible lighter of the candle
whose light corrodes your chin?

Which companions of the years
slapped or harried your profile
into its final, severe swerve,
pushed your brow to such feeling?

2.

As a young man
With a beret
With curly hair and white collar
As a young man

Open-mouthed as if shouting
Leaning forward
In a cap laughing
With dishevelled hair

Leaning on a stone sill
With a cap pulled forward
In soft hat and a patterned cloak
In cap and dark cloak

With two circles
In oriental attire
With bittern
With gorget and beret

With helmet
With beret and gold chain
With beret and two gold chains
Wide-eyed and open-mouthed

With raised sabre
With raised sabre
As the Apostle Paul
In a cloak with a falling collar

Whose fading beauty and passion
put the look in your eye,
that can seem arrogance, or affront
or sadness, but may be merely reeling?

Bareheaded
In cap and scarf with face dark
In cap and scarf with face dark
At the age of 63

What words say

Extracted from a Miriam Webster list of words first recorded in 1600, and words first recorded in 1962, the year of my birth

1600

Semi-divine   sumptuary—
unruffled,   raw-boned,
diffusive, probably.
Everblooming.   Green-eyed.
        Impolitic.
Beachy fairyland—
amused (conscious diversion)!
Floating, inside-
out.   Gazelle   giraffe   dumpling.

1962

Dystopian
kissing disease.

Prefaded
paraprofessional
peacenik.

Win-win
care-package,
degradable
fishfinger.

Herstory.

Basis-point
fudge factor.
Speed-reading
mini-skirt
expat!

Trendy
sitcom
body count.

Log-on,
bossa nova.

Twelfth Night

Gossamer shrouds the pine needles. Lustrous, night-spun garland swags to the curtain rail, mists each silvered bauble, dulls the pendant brass. A caul is plastered upon the painted eyes of the nutcracker, soft finery's laced to the splintery plumage of a bristlebird. We hauled the tree, fragrant and weeping, to fill the front room with the memory of scent. The spiders were there already. Upon this adorned scaffold, the small cavern of an angel's porcelain ear is no different to any resin-dark crack. Now we strip tinsel, tease ornaments free from hushing dry needles, prepare the remains for landfill, tell ourselves that the spiders' small, violable world remains intact.

Remaking scenery

If a boulder is needed
it can be made available—
as a seat on the mountain crest
for triumphant resting, as a weight
needing shifting,
as a symbol of defeat or a comic
threat, teetering.

Cattle, being biddable,
are easily inserted at any point—
to gaze long, graze with the rhythmic
ripping of a soft snare,
to turn presciently
against advancing weather
or loom as large, warm backdrop
to manger or stable.

A waterfall may be useful.
Romance and danger,
it rises like lightning
in all lights
from the boulder it strikes
with such clamour, painful whiteness,
such a spasm of sparks.
A waterfall can mean
almost anything,
is useful to end on.

First and final call

At this time we invite to board
all those who cannot say
if there will be anyone to meet them
at their destination.

We now welcome the weary of heart
—with baggage and without—
the disappointed in love,
the recently redundant.

We ask to remain patient those with
half-moons of holiday sunburn
at the tops of their thighs, and men
who can wear linen
for the long-haul without dishevelment.

This is the first and final call
for *un*believers and *dis*believers,
both the quiet and the indignant.
We apologise for the delay

and can now confirm your exit-row seats.
In the event of an emergency
we now, and at all times,
welcome unaccompanied infants.

Afterword

It seems almost remiss, in a year of inferno and pestilence—when masks filtering out bushfire particulates were briefly doffed, only to be replaced by masks shielding from a lethal airborne virus—to offer up a volume of poetry that reflects directly upon neither of these consuming concerns.

In extenuation I can only say that even those of my poems which are written 'quickly' generally have a long gestation period, conceived as indecipherable squiggles in notebooks, random lines, a phrase, a bookmarked link to a news story, a disembodied title, before they irritate their way to the surface and assert themselves.

That is not to say that the poems found here are entirely unconnected with the human behaviours that give rise to the times in which we live—in particular, our blithe and childlike trust that we humans can continue to pursue our rapacious, current path on this planet without self-awareness or—more importantly—consequence.

Notes

'Voucher Specimen', p.12

In 2015, *Audubon* magazine published the first photographs of the elusive male Guadalcanal moustached kingfisher https://www.audubon.org/news/moustached-kingfisher-photographed-first-time . The photographs were taken, in the Solomon Islands, by an American Museum of Natural History team. The team also captured and 'collected' a male kingfisher to serve as a 'voucher specimen' (a preserved example that serves as a verifiable record of a species). Disquiet from readers led *Audubon* to update its article to make it clearer that the bird had been euthanized, and the lead scientist wrote a second article in a later issue, explaining the decision to collect the specimen https://www.audubon.org/news/why-i-collected-moustached-kingfisher . This poem draws on these articles.

'Likenesses', p.80

1. Thích Quảng Đức, a Vietnamese Mahayana Buddhist monk, self-immolated in Saigon on 11 June 1963 to draw attention to the persecution of Buddhists by the South Vietnamese government of Ngô Đình Diệm. Malcolm Browne was awarded a Pulitzer Prize for his photograph of Đức's death. This poem draws in part on a 2011 Time interview with Browne https://time.com/3791176/malcolm-browne-the-story-behind-the-burning-monk/

2. Kevin Carter won a 1993 Pulitzer Prize for his photograph of a starving South Sudanese child with a vulture ominously poised in the background. The image was published in the New York Times. Some readers were horrified that Carter had not intervened to save the child. Some months later, in July 1994, Carter killed himself, writing that he was haunted by the memories of things he had photographed in Africa. http://100photos.time.com/photos/kevin-carter-starving-child-vulture

3. On 31 August 1997, Diana, Princess of Wales, the former wife of the heir to the British throne, died in a car crash in a Paris tunnel. The driver of the car was apparently fleeing 'paparazzi' at the time—freelance photographers who specialise in photographing high-profile people in their private lives. In 2008, three French paparazzi who took pictures of the crash scene were each fined a symbolic €1 by the French legal system for invasion of privacy.

Acknowledgments

Profound thanks to Michael Wellham, Paul Hetherington and Martin Dolan for reading and providing wise counsel regarding an early draft of this book, and to Russ Erwin, Bob Hefner, Virginia Cook and Neil Lade for their generous readings of and commentary upon individual poems. This book is better for your collective wisdom and your unstinting friendship.

Deep gratitude (again) to Recent Work Press publisher Shane Strange for believing there is still a place for poetry on our tongues and on our bookshelves, and for making a narrow space for mine.

A number of these poems, or versions of them, have been previously published in print and online journals.

Tabula rasa (*Not Very Quiet* 2019)
Antarctic (*The Canberra Times* 2020)
Drowned Town (*Rochford Street Review* 2019)
Survivalist (*Rochford Street Review* 2019)
Showtime (*These Strange Outcrops* - Cicerone anthology of Canberra writing 2020)
Blue Poles [Number 11, 1952] (*Cordite* 2017)
Every single piece of plastic ever made still exists, scientists say (*Western Humanities Review* 2018)
Insatiable (*Western Humanities Review* 2018)
Ruin porn (*Verity La* 2020)
Somnia (*Verity La* 2020)
Alice at the book depository (*Pulse* Prose Poems 2016)
Sympathy (*Pulse* Prose Poems 2016)
Scintilla (*Cordite* 2019)
Quaking Aspens, Utah (*Plumwood Mountain* 2020)
Communion (*Not Very Quiet* 2020)
The succession of forest trees (*Australian Poetry Anthology* 2020)
Ink (*The Blue Nib* 2020)
Naked on the street side (*The Blue Nib* 2020)
During a blackout (*Well-known Corners*, Canberra International Poetry Festival)

www.ingramcontent.com/pod-product-compliance
Lightning Source LLC
Chambersburg PA
CBHW020328010526
44107CB00054B/2019